HOW TO BE A 5-STAR RESELLER

A REALISTIC GUIDE TO EARNING MONEY

JAMES WILSON II

Copyright © 2019 JamesJiggyG LLC

All rights reserved. This book or any portion of this book may not be reproduced or used in any manner whatsoever without the express written permission of the publisher with the exception of brief quotations in a book review.

JamesJiggyG LLC

17120 Highway 72

Arvada, CO 80007

www.jamesjiggyg.com

Dedication

This book is dedicated to Marshall and Terri
for giving me a place to call "home" when I was
homeless. You've treated me like family and for that,
I'm forever grateful.

Table of Contents

Introduction vii

Chapter One: Introduction to Reselling 1

Chapter Two: What to Buy and Sell 5

Chapter Three: In Person Transactions 8

Chapter Four: Where to Buy and Sell 14

Chapter Five: Keys to Selling 20

Chapter Six: Scaling Your Business 27

Closing 31

Introduction

In this booklet I'm going to teach you the fundamentals of reselling. By the time you're finished reading, you'll know what reselling entails, what you should buy and sell, how to handle transactions, where to buy and sell, keys to selling, how to scale your business, and more! The contents of this booklet contain knowledge that I acquired during the hundreds of interactions I had with reselling. I wanted to share my knowledge and a few stories with you.

As you're reading, you'll find out how I made $35,000 in six months from reselling. I managed to accomplish that by starting with only $50. This is a realistic guide to earning money with reselling. There's no "fluff" in this booklet, just real knowledge and real results.

The resell game is becoming increasingly more difficult due to everyone and their mom doing it. That's not to say that you can't still earn money! There's opportunity everywhere! If you use the things I teach, you'll stand out above the crowd and excel. Consider this your pocket guide to earning money with reselling. There's no limit to how much you can earn!

CHAPTER ONE:

Introduction to Reselling

Before we get into earning money with reselling, I'm going to explain what reselling is. Reselling and "flipping" will be used interchangeably within this book. They're essentially the same thing. Reselling is a great way to start building capital for another venture. It's also a business that you can start with little to no capital, if you decide to pursue it as a business. Reselling is basically buying an item or several items and selling them at a profit (or loss, depending). Obviously, the concept is to buy at a price that you can make profit on the items later, when selling.

The nice thing about starting a resell business is that you can literally start with no money! If you have no available funds, you can search Craigslist for free items and start there. You can actually find some pretty nice stuff in the free section. If you don't want to start there, you can always start off by selling some items that you already own and no longer need or use. Another way to start with no money is to keep your eyes and ears open! People are always giving stuff away or throwing goods out. Take advantage! Don't be embarrassed to ask for the items being given away or to grab something off the street, in front of a house with a "free" sign on it. This could be the start to something big!

If you think people only give away "junk," you're wrong! I've seen Craigslist ads with people giving away expensive furniture because they were moving and didn't want to haul it. Sometimes people give stuff away because they don't want to be inconvenienced. Other times it's because they don't use it anymore. Everyone has their own reasons to give stuff away. The reason doesn't matter, capitalize on it!

Just for grins, I just looked at the free ads on Craigslist to give you some examples. The very first thing listed is several wood pallets. This might seem insignificant but you can sell wood pallets for $5-$20 each in the area I live. It depends on the pallet type and quality. The next thing on the list is a solid wood desk. You could easily clean it, sand it, stain it, and make money on it. Scrolling through quickly, I see several working appliances, doors, windows, furniture, and more. Just glancing through the first page, someone reselling these free items could make $500 pretty easily. Granted you need to be able to store and haul the items. This just goes to show you that opportunity is everywhere for people willing to take the initiative to do something about it!

Reselling is simple. You buy items at prices that you think you can make profit on when selling. For example, you buy a bicycle in great shape for $100. You only buy the bicycle if you know that you can make profit on it. In the beginning it's speculation. Eventually, you gain an understanding of the value of things and become a better judge when purchasing. If you're unsure, do research before buying! It's easy to quickly research nowadays with cell phones. Generally speaking, you'll become an expert on a specific product or niche, then concentrate your efforts on those items. Even when you become an expert on something specific, you want to pay attention to anything and everything that can make you a decent profit. It's up to you to decide what you consider a worthy profit. When I first started reselling, I was happy making $5 profit on one item. Eventually, I wouldn't even buy something unless I could make at least $50 on it. The biggest step in earning money from reselling is to start! Stop thinking about it and do it! You're never going to be an expert on everything but the more you resell, the more you know about the items and what makes money. Get out and start!

CHAPTER TWO:

What to Buy and Sell

This is a question I've been asked several times from people just starting to resell. "What should I be buying?" The answer to that is going to vary, depending on the person. If you're already an expert in shoes or know quite a bit about shoes, buy and sell shoes! If you have a collection of Star Wars figures and know a lot about Star Wars, buy and sell Star Wars items! Know a ton about guitars? You guessed it, concentrate your efforts on reselling guitars! People tend to overthink things and worry about what is selling. Trust me when I say that people are buying everything. If you are educated on a product or niche, concentrate on that. If the hottest selling product this month is designer purses but you don't know jack crap about designer purses, you'll fail miserably trying to resell them. It doesn't matter if it's the hottest selling item or not. More than likely you're going to buy a "fake" and get hosed. If you don't know about it, don't buy it. Concentrate on what you know, in the beginning at least.

When first starting out, don't worry about buying expensive, more profitable items. The more you get familiar with products, the more money you'll make. If you're just getting into the resell game, I'd focus on lower priced items to minimize risk and get a feel for things. Say you decide to resell acoustic guitars. Don't go out and spend $1000 on a Martin or Taylor. For one, there are limited number of people that are willing to buy a used guitar for that much money. Second, you'll be sitting on that $1000 purchase until you sell it, which could be awhile. Focus your efforts toward low to mid-range price points. You'll be able to sell a middle of the road Taylor quicker than a higher end version. Not to mention you'll still stand to make a good profit, assuming you bought at a good price. "You make money when you buy, not when you sell."

When you do figure out what you want to buy and sell, jump on opportunities quickly! If you see that an ad was just posted two hours ago and it's a killer deal, make the deal happen. You're not the only one trying to make deals. There are more people reselling now than ever before! You have to capitalize on opportunity! Make sure you always have cash on hand. This is a mistake I see a lot of people make. If you have to go by the bank to get cash and person B doesn't. The seller will sell to the first person that shows up, more than likely. Have cash on hand!

CHAPTER THREE:

In Person Transactions

First off, be safe! Fortunately, I've always had very good interactions with people. Just as a precaution, I always carry a Glock 9mm too, in case things don't go smoothly. I'm not trying to scare you off from reselling but there are bad people in the world. As a reseller that's always interacting with strangers, it's better to be safe than sorry. Always meet in public spaces and be smart about who you're doing business with. If something seems "off," don't meet them. You can always buy or sell from someone else.

I'm going to give you some tips, when buying. When buying something to resell, always negotiate prices! You'd be surprised what people are willing to sell stuff for. I personally like to negotiate beforehand so there are no surprises when we meet. Some people prefer to negotiate in person, which is okay too. I also like to create a sense of urgency to the seller. I like to send messages that say something like this, "John, I saw your scroll saw on craigslist. Will you take $50 cash? I'll pick it up tonight. Thanks, James." This message example is simple and straight to the point. I like to include a link to the ad or at least the name of what they're selling. A lot of sellers have multiple items listed. It's easier for them to know which product you're referring to. In the above scenario, we'll assume he's asking $100 for the saw. I start off with the seller's name to make the message personable. Then, I offer what I'm willing to pay and I make sure to include that I'll be giving him cash. Lastly, I create a sense of urgency by saying I'll pick it up tonight or at a specific time. This shows that you're serious about buying and willing to meet. There are so many "flaky" people online that many sellers are willing to take a lesser amount, just to know someone will actually show up! Always end the message with your name. This shows that you're a real person and makes it more personable.

The seller will agree to your offer more times than not. Assuming that you didn't "lowball" too much. Occasionally, you'll have someone counteroffer. You'll have to decide what you're willing to pay. If they counteroffer and you still stand to make a good profit, accept. If you're not comfortable paying the counteroffer, then propose your own counter. If you can't come to an agreement, just thank them and walk away. Don't take anything personally! If we can't come to an agreement, I like to tell them to keep my information and to reach out when they are ready to sell. You'd be surprised how many people will reach out in a week or two. I can't stress this enough, don't take it personally! So many people get bent out of shape when they don't get their way. I've been called every name under the sun. Those idiots just get blocked and accomplish nothing.

When you set a time to meet, keep your word! There's nothing worse than talking to someone for a few hours about something they're buying or selling, just to drive to the meeting location and they don't show up. Keep your word! I also make it a point to respond to the other person as quick as possible. It shows that you're serious and dependable. Even if you're reselling for "side income," be professional. You don't have to dress overly nice for a meeting but I'd recommend being presentable. You never know who you're going to meet. They might end up being someone that you sell a lot of stuff to or someone that has some great opportunity for you. You never know! I had one guy that reached out to me almost weekly to find stuff for him. I probably made $2000 off of just him.

When you finally reach the point where you're at the location and ready to meet, be polite. The first thing you should do when you see the person is smile and say "hi." Or a variation of that. Then, shake their hand! Introduce yourself! Those few things will make the transaction go very well!

More times than not, you'll end up talking for a bit about whatever and may even gain a new contact or friend. Personally, I always give them my business card before I leave. Upon departure, I shake their hand again and thank them. You have everything to gain from being kind to people.

Notes

CHAPTER FOUR:

Where to Buy and Sell

There are so many places to shop for products to resell! I have the best luck on Craigslist and LetGo, for both buying and selling. Although, I've found some amazing stuff at Goodwill and other thrift stores. Places like Marshalls can also have items worthy of buying for resell. I've also won my fair share of storage auctions. Storage units can be profitable but you also get a lot of junk. Make sure you have a place to store everything! I've also ordered bulk items from wholesalers, etc. Don't limit yourself to one place. You should always keep your eyes and ears open to opportunity. It really doesn't matter where you buy, as long as you're buying for a price worthy of making a decent profit.

I'll tell you about some of the places I've bought from and what I sold those items for. I bought ten pairs of Jordan's and Adidas at Marshalls for around $20 a pair. I turned around and sold them fairly quickly on LetGo and Craigslist for anywhere between $40-$100 a pair, depending on their market value. There was a time I was driving home and decided to stop by a Goodwill really quick. I walked in and spotted a Natural Light metal sign on the wall, almost instantly. I grabbed it, looked around a bit, and walked out. I paid $2 for the sign. I sold it within the week for $150 on Ebay. I'll take a $148 profit, any day!

I once paid $50 for a 5x5 storage unit in downtown Denver. The only reason I bid on it was because there was a fixed gear bike on the top of everything. I knew I could easily sell it for $100 or more. Almost everything in the unit was junk with the exception of the bike, that I sold for $150. The other good find was a genuine Gucci watch that retailed for $1300. I decided to keep it but I could have sold it for $500 fairly easily.

Deals are everywhere! I found two Taylor Big Baby guitars in pristine condition on Craigslist, the same day. They were asking $200 for each of them. I talked them down to $100 cash for each. I went and picked them up, listed them, and had them sold the next day for $250 each. I made $300 profit on that one deal (minus gas expenses). The best moment of sales I had at one time was in a Target parking lot in Arvada, Colorado. I met a few people there, all within thirty minutes of one another. I sold a couple bikes and a couple guitars. I walked away with $1000 profit. I had about an hour invested in those deals.

Personally, I like to meet everyone in person and do cash deals. I'd prefer to meet someone in a random parking lot and walk away with $100 cash than sell something online. Some of the common places I would sell stuff included Craigslist, Let-Go, Ebay, work, Offerup, and to random friends.

Ebay was nice because you could reach a big audience but I hated shipping stuff and paying the associated fees. At one time, I had two "power seller" accounts on ebay and was spending a stupid amount of time packaging, driving to the post office, and shipping everything. It was nice to be selling so much but it was too big of an inconvenience compared to the profits, so I wasn't a fan. Not to mention, I had several shelves full of boxes, tape, and packaging supplies. Ebay can be a good venue but inconvenient at the same time.

A lot of the people that bought stuff from me were work colleagues or friends. It's surprising how many people you know want to buy things you're selling! If they're looking for something specific, they'll start asking you to look for them too. This is an awesome opportunity! You already know you have a buyer; you just have to find a good price and seller.

I only sold a couple things through Offerup. It sucked for the most part. Like I said, Craigslist and LetGo were my go-to venues for buying and selling! They're easy and convenient. You can literally lay in bed and make deals happen. There are no fees associated with either platform (unless you "boost" your listing). They both have a large amount of people using their platforms, so plenty of people are seeing your listings. Obviously the bigger the city you're in, the more people that are going to see your listings.

If you're in a thrift store or some type of wholesale store and there are resellers everywhere, don't be discouraged! It's easy to look around and see that other people are looking for goods to resell too. Just because they're looking doesn't mean that they have the same knowledge that you do. The more you know, the more you'll earn and the better deals you'll find.

I've walked right behind an obvious reseller at Goodwill in the past and literally found an entire cart full of high-end clothing that he didn't know the value of. I'm talking about Brioni, Ermenegildo Zegna, and Thomas Pink dress shirts. Perhaps, he did know the value but didn't want to try to sell it. You never know what peoples reasoning is but it doesn't matter, capitalize! I've also passed up a fake Gucci handbag in a thrift store, just to see another reseller with less knowledge, smiling ear to ear because of their "find." Learn more and be the best!

CHAPTER FIVE:

Keys to Selling

There are some huge tips I'm going to share in this chapter! Your listings can sell themselves if done properly. So many people are too lazy to make their listings stand out or even decent, for that matter. You've all seen the crappy ads with horrible quality photos, no photos, or bad descriptions. Sometimes, all the above apply. Don't rush your listing!

If I had to pick one thing that can make you or break you in reselling, it's your listing quality. Always post photos! Don't be lazy. Take your time taking product photos! Don't just quickly snap with your cell phone and post. Make sure that your lighting is good, frame the product, then snap the photo. After you take the photo, edit it, and crop it. I always used my cell phone, although I have a DSLR. It's just more convenient and works well for resell photos. I used the Photoshop Express app to edit and crop. You don't have to do an elaborate edit, just adjust your highlights, white balance, sharpness, etc. People will pay more money for something if it has quality photos. I frequently took advantage of this when buying. You can buy at lower prices because of a crappy listing that no one else wants.

Aside from having a few quality photos at different angles, you should have a good main image. This is important! You want people to be enticed to click on your listing. Make sure your listing title is descriptive but simple. Capitalize your title too, if you feel necessary. Here's an example of an effective title: STATE BICYCLE CO. FIXED GEAR (FLIP/FLOP HUB). This title is simple, states the brand, explains what is for sale and a feature that someone may want. Simple and effective!

Make sure your listing has a good description! No one is going to be enticed to buy something from you if your description says "Cool guitar." The description doesn't have to be long but it should at least be descriptive (imagine that)! Be sure to list the condition of the item, along with the features and benefits. Don't copy and paste the description from another website. It's okay to do this after you write your own description but don't just copy and paste only. It's lazy and ineffective. It never hurts to end the listing with a call to action and your name! "Available now, text James at ###-###-####."

Congratulations! You now have a professional listing that will get attention! To recap, you want a good main photo, quality photos of different angles, effective title, good description, call to action, and your name and contact info.

If you focus your effort on one niche or a couple different niches, you'll start encountering people that are looking for stuff within those niches. If you don't currently have what they're looking for, build a clientele list! The main two niches I focused on were bicycles and guitars. I can't tell you how many times I would have people reach out to me via e-mail, LetGo, Craigslist, or in person, looking for an item I didn't have. I would jot down their information and tell them I would look for them and let them know if I came up with something.

I'll show you how effective a clientele list can be! There was a bicycle listed online for $250. I noticed the bike had been listed for several months. I sent the seller a message and said "Tim, Will you take $150 cash? I'll pick it up any time after 3p. Thanks, James" He replied and said "No." Instead of taking his response personally, I sent him a reply and said "Thanks for the quick response! Let me know when you're willing to consider my offer. Thanks, James" About a month later, he reached out and said "I'll do $150, if you're still interested?" At this point, the listing had been posted for a year at $250. I told him I was still interested and we arranged a meeting. I met him in a grocery store parking lot and handed him the $150 cash. As he was walking away, I was taking photos on my cell phone, against my vehicle. I had five people wanting that size bicycle. I sent them all the photos I had just taken and before the previous seller had even made it out of the parking lot, I had it sold for $250. This goes to show you how effective a clientele list can be. Matching a buyer with a product they're looking for can be easy money.

You're probably reading the above story and saying "Yeah, right! Why wouldn't your buyer just buy it online to begin with?" People are lazy! My buyer didn't want to take the time to find what he wanted. He'd rather have me do it, so I did! Even if he did look, he might not look all of the places that I look. Put in the work and your efforts will pay off.

When potential buyers send you messages about a product or call you, be sure to evaluate their words and expressions. If someone sends a message that says "I LOVE the guitar you have

HOW TO BE A 5-STAR RESELLER

listed! Would you be willing to knock $25 off?" I can quickly see that they really want the guitar! Therefore, I'll play hardball and tell them that the listed price is the best that I can do. Most times, with a message like the one above, they'll pay full price. The same goes for buying something! Be careful with how you present yourself. It makes a difference in the pricing and negotiations. If you show that you're willing to walk away or don't necessarily need the item, you'll have the control. Negotiations are about control. The person that's most willing to walk away will be triumphant.

When selling big or heavy products, it makes the most sense to sell locally because of shipping costs. With small products, you have the choice to sell locally or to ship the goods. It's up to you to decide what works best for you. I like to list the item I'm selling on as many platforms as possible to maximize the number of potential buyers seeing it. Once again, don't be lazy! It takes a little more time and effort to list in multiple places but it's worth it! You'll sell faster and for more money, generally.

After you sell a product, get into the habit of asking for feedback. Not everyone is going to take the time, but a lot of people will! Make sure you ask for feedback! It's crucial to build trust with potential buyers. Buying is based on emotions, more times than not. If you're a trustworthy seller with lots of good feedback, you'll improve your chances of selling! Ebay gives you a "power seller" badge, which helps increase your sales. Even on LetGo, there is a 5-star rating system. I always ask for a 5-star rating! By responding quickly, being polite, and showing up on time, I have a perfect rating on both Ebay and Letgo. Trust is very important in sales!

CHAPTER SIX:

Scaling Your Business

The time will eventually come when you'll want to start making more money! That could mean overall or per item. Reselling is a pretty easy business to scale. It takes the same time and effort to flip a flatbed trailer online as it does a name brand dress shirt. The difference is the amount of profit you're going to get from each. The shirt might make you $15 profit. The trailer could make you $500 or more, depending. This is why scaling is important!

The most common way to scale is by buying and selling more expensive and more profitable items. The more time you spend reselling, the more comfortable you'll become with it. You'll get an idea of what sells and what doesn't. It's surprising how much knowledge you gain about random products, fairly quickly. You may start by being an expert in shoes. After a year of reselling, you may be reselling cars and super knowledgeable about them. You gain a basic knowledge of everything, honestly. After six months of reselling, I could walk into a thrift store, close my eyes and feel through the neckties and tell you which ones were handmade in Italy and an expensive brand. Prior to reselling, I knew nothing about necktie quality.

The more you resell and become comfortable, the more money you'll be willing to spend to make money. You might start with no money in the beginning, then resell so much that you're able to afford to flip cars (although it's illegal in a lot of states, check with your local laws). The difference in profit depends on the items you sell.

When I first started reselling, I was doing it to build capital for a business that I wanted to start. I hardly had any money in the beginning. I might've had $50 to spend. Not knowing what I was doing, I just started buying anything and everything that I thought I could make a profit on. I went through the initial $50 quickly. I started selling a couple items, here and there. I was making about $5 profit per item sold. Some of the things never sold. I just donated them.

Quickly, I realized that making $5 per item was unsustainable, not to mention it sucked. I was putting in so much time and effort, just to get a little more. I knew I needed to scale. About the time I realized I needed to make more profit per item, I had a work colleague that was looking for a bicycle. Long story short, I found him a bike. I paid $50 for it and sold it to him the next day for $125, if I remember correctly. I made a super quick $75 on that one transaction. I knew enough about bikes, so I decided to start focusing my efforts toward reselling bikes. Around the same time, I decided to flip guitars as well.

After making the decision to focus on bikes and guitars, I started to make some serious cash! I made anywhere from $50-$200 profit per item. It reached a point where I wouldn't even buy something unless I made at least $50 on it. It was no longer worth my time. I liked the price point of the bikes and guitars. They didn't take a lot of money out of my pocket and they were quick to sell. That's the recipe for getting money from reselling! I'd rather sit on a product a couple of days and make $50 than sit on it a year and make $1000.

Closing

In my first six months of reselling, I made $35,000 profit. I still worked a full-time job too. I was reselling on the side, after work and on my days off. Business was the best on the weekends, I noticed. That makes sense, considering a lot of people are off work. I quickly made the money I needed to start my business and moved on to other ventures. The amount I learned from those reselling days was worth a ton!

I hope you found the information in this booklet useful! For more financial education, visit jamesjiggyg.com. Sign up for the mailing list to be the first to know about new books, discounts, new blogs, and more! Please leave a positive review on Amazon, if you found this booklet helpful! If you think it sucked, leave a review telling me and everyone else why! Thanks for reading. Slay the day!

Notes

www.ingramcontent.com/pod-product-compliance
Lightning Source LLC
Chambersburg PA
CBHW070843220526
45466CB00002B/864